CREATIVE REBOOT

Unlock Your Creative Potential
for a Deeper, More Meaningful Life
in Less Than 15 Minutes a Day

OSVALDO QUINTANILLA

For information contact;

hello@osvaldoquintanilla.com

www.osvaldoquintanilla.com

Book and Cover design by Osvaldo Quintanilla

ISBN: 978-1522938668

First Edition: January 2016

10 9 8 7 6 5 4 3 2 1

Dedication

I dedicate this book to my grandmother Elba Lobos
who from my earliest memories encouraged me to look at
everyday things differently, be curious and set me on the
path of creativity.

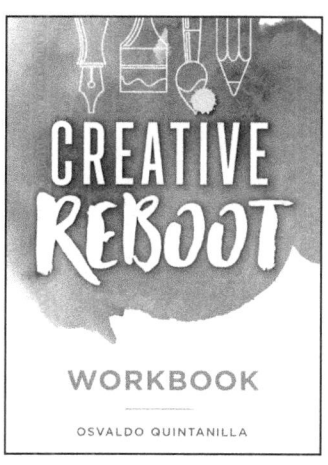

DOWNLOAD THE CREATIVE REBOOT WORKBOOK FREE!

To compliment the *Creative Reboot* a FREE Workbook
is available to download from:

**www.osvaldoquintanilla.com/
creative-reboot-workbook/**

To get the most out of this book use this workbook as
you read. I encourage you to print it out so you get a
feeling of working with pen and paper. The workbook
will enhance the exercises and give you something to
look back on and see how far you have come.

There's a little more inspiration and fun stuff in the
workbook to keep you going too.

CONTENTS

INTRODUCTION

So you have been thinking about doing something creative but never get the time or inspiration to start. Would you like to do something for yourself and express your own creativity? Maybe you used to like drawing when you were young, but as you got older other things became more important. Or perhaps your work is busy and you just never seem to find the time. Does this sound like you?

If you are one of these people who have been putting off doing something creative because it's too hard then this book is for you. In easy to follow steps, you will learn how to start the creative process in your busy life no matter how much or how little time you think you have. This book has been designed to show you how to find the time to be creative, find your own creative skills, and finally build your own creative life that will be fulfilling in so many ways.

As a graphic designer working for more than twenty years Osvaldo has explored many ways of being creative in his daily life: from screen printing through furniture design and drawing to writing fiction. His experience of working in busy and demanding roles has taught him how to consistently come up with new ideas when needed, and most importantly how to balance his time between work and his own creative projects. He is passionate about the creative process and knows how fulfilling and ultimately satisfying it is to pursue your own creativity.

By following the steps and doing the exercises in this book you will find your creativity will increase dramatically. You will learn proven inspiration techniques that are easy to do and be able to draw on your new-found inspiration whenever you need it. The end result will be that your creative ideas become reality. Learn the techniques and tips in easy to follow steps and see how you can fit it into your work/life balance.

So stop thinking about doing that creative hobby, or how you want to do something more fulfilling one day. Don't leave the opportunity to have a creative life to chance. Be the kind of person that knows how to turn on their creativity when they need to. To have creative projects running alongside your work life and relish in the knowledge you can do both without sacrificing your life. Become the productive creative person you see in other 'talented' people, who has ideas bursting from you. Start today by reading the following chapter, where you learn the first method to creative life: knowing how to be open to creativity.

Make time to start your creative life right now and create a happier, more fulfilling life along the way.

How did creativity begin for me?

I was born in a small town in Chile called San Felipe. The town lies between Santiago and the Andes mountains and I lived there until I was five years old. Chile was going through a lot of political unrest during the early 1970s. The country had experienced a coup where a dictator named Pinochet had come to power and with that change, fear and uncertainty came into people's lives. As a result the economy suffered badly and jobs were hard to come by. My parents scraped by to provide the basics at home and not much more.

What does any of this have to do with being creative you might be wondering? I guess it sets the scene for the climate in which I grew up – a time when my parents didn't travel very much, or have the money to buy many toys. In fact I do remember only two toys I had from that time: a wind up tin car that flipped over and sped back in the opposite direction and a wind up robot that had a plastic television in its chest.

I was an only child until the age of nine, which meant I had to find ways of keeping myself busy and interested in the world around me. Our house had a large backyard with fruit trees and many rose bushes which were my grandmother's pride and joy. It was in that setting that I remember playing games, or creating make-believe scenarios.

Around that time, perhaps when I was three or four years old, I started drawing, I assume because paper and pencils were cheap and it was the easiest way for my parents to keep me entertained. Often the scenes I drew were re-enactments of things I had seen on TV – cowboys and Indians, jet planes or pirates on the seas.

One scene remains vividly in my mind – a certain Jacques Cousteau documentary appeared on TV one day. The footage of men in their rubber suits and breathing tanks exploring the depths of the oceans captivated me and of course I immediately replayed the scenes on paper.

I was so consumed by these documentaries that I would draw them again and again, adding new details each time, depending on what I had seen in the latest Jacques Cousteau film that day.

Now I look back on that time and see that the things I was learning through those childish exercises was the basis of being creative. When you are limited in your scope, and you adopt one medium with persistence, and are inspired to explore one theme over and over again, the result is a surge in creative skill and ability – which some people call talent.

In actual fact I think it's more about honing a skill through persistence. This doesn't have the same romantic notion as 'talent' I guess, but nonetheless we all improve our skills in life. Most of the time we aren't aware that we are doing it.

Drawing became my thing. I found the more I drew the things that interested me, the better my drawings became and so I drew more of the things around me. That desire to explore through drawing, painting or writing has never disappeared. It's just part of my life and feels natural to delve into it whenever I need to.

Becoming a graphic designer was a natural progression from the hobbies and passions that I enjoyed as a kid. Today in my job I am always on the lookout for new and visually exciting things as part of my everyday life. I don't intentionally look for that 'something' that inspires me; it's just how I've come to observe the world.

It might be in a flea market or a second hand store, it could be a book, or a trinket or an object that stops me in my tracks. I will often buy that thing, as I know it will be useful for a creative project sometime in the future. More often than not, I have no idea what that creative project will be, but I know it has some inspiring value so I have to have it. This natural curiosity has helped me in my work as a graphic designer.

How do creative people find that new and unique solution every time? Well, a lot of it for me comes down firstly to being a curious person. Curiosity is the starting point for any creative solution – I am always asking why something is made that way, or why something is that color. In this way I can uncover a hidden truth that might provide me with the answer I can use for my own creativity.

I mention all these personal experiences to demonstrate how my own life has been a journey of constant learning and doing. In this book I have brought together all these experiences to create a guideline and process that anyone can follow. If you are one of those people who wants to increase your own creative activity; whether it's painting, photography or writing and get the most out it in your personal life, the steps and methods in the following chapters will help you achieve this.

Of course, your experience will be unique, depending where you have come from and your own journey will shape your creative direction. As I have found, once you are actively on your creative path, your life will be enriched and fulfilled in ways that will surprise and delight you.

This book is put together in such a way that it takes you on a journey. It will help ease you toward a creative lifestyle. The rewards are there for the reader who is patient and willing to do the exercises consistently. Creativity after all can't happen overnight.

Each chapter will give you a new insight about the creative process and build on the last chapter. These are important to build the basic building blocks for your own creative life going forward.

Why 15 minutes? We all have busy lives. No matter how much we know doing something for ourselves is good for our well-being, it's hard to get going sometimes. That's why all the exercises in this book can be done in 15 minute or less intervals. That way you can feel it's an achievable goal. Of course if you want to spend more time being creative that's highly encouraged too!

Change your outlook, change your life

Today, when people ask me what I do for a living and I answer I'm a graphic designer, they often say, 'Oh, you must be really good at drawing'. And quickly follow with, 'I used to love to draw as a child'. Then they go on to explain that now that as an adult they have lost all ability to be artistic.

At this point I tell them that the reality of a graphic designer in our modern age is more about moving a mouse on a desk than putting a pencil to paper. But I do make a point of saying that the tool all graphic designers use every day is their creativity.

This skill is somehow viewed as a mysterious thing by people who say, 'I don't have a creative bone in my body'. The truth is, everyone has creative potential. All children have an innate creative ability – you only have to watch them play or draw to see that – but most people don't keep using it as they grow up. Perhaps it's our rational world that slowly takes over and vanquishes that creative desire over time.

The more I come in contact with people from all fields of work the more I realise we all have a desire to create in whatever form feels right to us. More often than not, people simply think creativity is too far out of reach for them. By keeping exercises to 15 minutes or less you will be able get on with being creative, find inspiration and develop a fulfilling creative life for yourself no matter how busy you are.

So if you've always had an inclination to paint, draw or write but keep putting it aside, now you have a way to start. By the end of this book you will know what works for you and what doesn't. You will have a feel for a particular media like paint, pencil or collage and know which one you want to pursue further.

So let's start by getting your mind into creative shape.

Finding what it means for you

Creativity ignites our passion. Who wants to live their lives devoid of passion and float through the world being indifferent? That's why we admire people who give passionate speeches like Martin Luther King or feel the emotion of the singer of a love song. We get inspired when we hear a chef speak passionately about food. That's because all these people are tapping into their own creativity and their passion flows from that.

When we have passion for something, in this case the passion to create something artistic, we tap into something deep inside us that has been yearning to be heard. We are able to give it all our energy because we know that passion is coming from somewhere real.

Creativity is an expression of our ideas, thoughts and inspirations. It helps us convey who we are in a way that is authentic and real. And when that happens we are being true to ourselves. Artists have striven for this for generations and as you embark on this journey, you will also find a place where you are being true to yourself.

Creativity helps us connect with people on an emotional level. And we inherently want to make connections with other people; it's just part of being human. You may know that feeling when someone has seen something you created and said 'Wow! You made this?' That warm and contented feeling at seeing their reaction comes from knowing you have connected with them emotionally. That could be a connection brought about by your painting, drawing or photography.

We instinctively want to create things; we just don't acknowledge it very often. And we don't nurture our own ability to create and hence be a creative person in our everyday life. For example when we day-dream about a new home, we are starting that creative process. In fact, day-dreaming is a natural way our minds work to come up with stuff.

Sometimes those ideas can become reality when we actively do practical things to make them happen. The same goes for creative projects that may start with a simple thought and develop from there.

As you begin this process it will help to think what are the reasons you want to be more creative. What's the purpose that makes you want to embark on this journey? You don't have to have the answer right now, but it will become clear along the way. Maybe you just want to paint, draw, or just have a creative outlet that balances your work life. Or you might feel you have something to express, but aren't sure exactly what that is yet.

Whatever the reasons, once you start the creative process, you will unconsciously bring new experiences into your life. Those experiences will be richer and you will absorb them into more ideas as you continue creating. This well of creativity will never run dry – it will keep giving more, the more you use it in your life.

Below are the steps that will start you on your creative journey.

Step 1. Let creativity into your life
Step 2. Create your space
Step 3. Cultivate Inspiration
Step 4. Work up Perspiration
Step 5. Stay on your path

STEP 1

LET CREATIVITY INTO YOUR LIFE

Every child is an artist. The problem is how to remain an artist once the child grows up.
– Pablo Picasso

CREATIVITY IN YOUR LIFE

As much as we would all like to just switch on our creativity, it doesn't work that way. In fact as soon as you say to yourself, 'Right. Now I'm going to do something creative' and sit down at your desk with pencil and paper, you'll probably stare at the blank paper without any inspiration coming to you. That type of frustration is likely to put you off for good.

Instead, you have to lay the foundation for the creativity to flow. Just like an athlete needs to warm up before running onto the field to perform at his best, so too you have to 'warm up' your mind to allow creative thoughts to come easily.

In this chapter you will learn all about limbering up the mind so that your creativity will begin to flow. But do resist the urge to jump ahead to the creative exercises, although I applaud your enthusiasm. You will get so much more out of this book by getting your mind ready first.

Keeping your thoughts positive

When you are beginning your creative life, it's all about building something new. The best way to encourage that building process is by inviting positivity into your life. Think about how people are affected in a workplace when they have negative thoughts about their job.

We all know that person who anytime we ask how their day is going will give you a list of problems and negative things that are happening to them. There isn't much hope for a person to do creative things who instead focuses on negativity. That's why from the very beginning you have to encourage your thoughts to be positive.

By steering your thoughts toward the positive, you will dispel all those negative thoughts that emerge when anyone of us starts something creative. They sound something like this: 'I don't have enough talent', 'I'm not as creative as...so and so', 'I can't draw', 'I'm not good at coming up with ideas', 'I'm not artistic'. (I could go on). Sound familiar? So how do you counteract this type of thinking if it's been something that's stopped you in the past?

When you acknowledge all the good things in your life, good things keep coming back to you in other ways and creativity flourishes on this type of thinking. For example, you could acknowledge your family and friends as positive influences in your life, but also think about your inner self. What things in your personality or behaviour right now are positive? Are you generous, or do you like to help others, make people laugh or encourage people?

Positive traits such as these work like a feedback loop; they will come back to feed your creativity in time. For example, by the act of giving your time and energy to others you will find that you will receive in return some day. It might be just what you need when you're feeling stuck on a creative project.

A positive mindset also creates a 'can do' attitude for any task you have to do. It's amazing how having this positive 'can do' approach can eliminate any fears when embarking on a new project.

You might think this exercise is a little self indulgent, but it's about being honest with yourself, not pumping up your ego and just listing wonderful things about you. Be realistic about the positive aspects you have, and acknowledge where you could change your view to be more positive. When you become aware of the positive in your life you will set the grounding for a more successful creative life.

Exercise 1. Acknowledging Positivity

Use the workbook to write a list of three positive things in your life when you get up in the morning. This could be a relationship, a friend, or a positive event that has happened recently.

As you begin to write, your mind will inevitably find a negative thought almost in opposition to what you have written. This is a good opportunity to be aware of these negative thoughts and to be able to dismiss them as not having relevance. In time you will find that that the negative thoughts become weaker and less and less relevant to you.

Throughout the day be aware of what you have written for the day, so when that co-worker begins to tell you all the negative stuff that's happening to him or her, you can be ready and not let it change your positive mindset. I've found this especially useful when things have become stressful at work by allowing me to take a step back before I become swept up in the negativity.

Try this exercise for 5 days in a row and see what things you discover about yourself.

Switch off

Some of you may not like this next part. Please stop watching TV. Yes, you read correctly. I'm not suggesting throwing out your TV; instead think of it as taking time out from each other. Right now I don't have a TV and although it wasn't a conscious decision, it's become part of my life. Occasionally I still find it hard when I get home from work and all I want to do is 'relax' in front of the box. The reason I've resisted the urge to buy one so far is because I've seen the difference it's made to my habits each evening.

As part of getting yourself into the right mind set, all you need to do is give up watching TV for 3-5 days. Especially important is to resist the urge to flop down on the couch when you get home from work and switch the box on. It's an incredible time zapper! You would be familiar with the scenario where you sit and say to yourself, 'I just need to 'tune out' for a few minutes then I'll do X', and before you know it two hours have passed and you can hardly remember what you just saw. The reason for this is that TV networks are experts at making you sit and watch their reality TV shows, sitcoms and news, one after another. That's their job.

Apart from taking time away from you, where you could be working on something creative, TV can fill you with anxiety and negative thoughts a lot of the time. As you know, when watching TV, inevitably you come across news events from around the country or the world that are sad or shocking to watch. Your mind is quickly filled with all sorts of terrible news that never seems to end. None of which is good for your creative process to begin.

There's nothing wrong with being knowledgeable about world events or politics, but there'll be plenty of time to catch up at a later stage. The constant cycle of bad news is not a good basis for your creative output. You want to be free from that type of influence at this time. The sad reality is that when you do go back to watching TV you will be back up to speed with current events in no time – the good and bad.

Try to avoid the box for 3 days at a time, then try 5 days straight. In your newly acquired time, you will find other things that keep you entertained such as listening to music you haven't played for a while, discovering a podcast on a new topic, or reading a book you have been putting off for a while. You don't have to avoid all media and current events altogether, as you'll probably still read a paper or hear the radio throughout the week, but at least you have broken the cycle of TV hypnosis.

You'll find that it's not such a big thing after the 5 days and perhaps you might even extend it for longer. You can allow yourself to watch specific TV shows you have on DVD or downloads as long as you keep them in small portions and they aren't taking up all your evenings. And of course going out to watch a movie is allowed.

Exercise 2. No TV? Now what?

You have now vanquished your TV set from your home. (By the way, you can cover it with a nice colorful fabric if that helps you keep it out of mind). Keep your workbook handy and at the end of each day you don't watch TV make a note of the things you did that you would not have done if you were watching TV. You might be surprised at the things you do in a week. Or you can make a note of the struggle you had giving up your TV viewing too.

Working with mindfulness

Once you have eliminated some of the distractions and negative things in your life, you will notice a change in your thoughts and perhaps a change in your view of the world around you.

This next part will build on those positive thoughts. Mindfulness and meditation are age-old eastern techniques. More recently western thinking has employed these techniques to work better, and enhance our well-being. Both mindfulness and meditation are often associated with creativity. Mindfulness is simply the state of being in the moment. Or put another way, keeping your thoughts in the present, not thinking about the future or the past. It can be done when you're brushing your teeth or having a shower. It teaches you to be present and aware of all your senses when you are doing that activity, not thinking about where you're going next and who you have to call.

You may have experienced a scenario where you have driven home and then not remembered much about the trip when you got there. Our minds are easily distracted and constantly narrating things to us that often aren't very important. The Buddhists call it the monkey mind that is always chattering.

Meditation is similar to mindfulness and can often be called mindfulness meditation. To practice it is very easy. You can do it in a chair or sit on a yoga mat; wherever is comfortable for you. Here the aim is to clear your thoughts and quieten your mind in the process. It can be a really great exercise to help de-stress or get clarity on certain creative problems you might have.

Why mindfulness works so well with creativity is because it helps you to be in the moment. Have you ever watched children draw or paint? Without trying they play and create in a state of mindfulness. When they draw a line or color in they are experiencing that action and not thinking about what they need to cook for dinner or the next day's work. But when we grow into adults our ability to stay in the moment is greatly reduced or disappears altogether. The great thing is you can reignite this state of being with practice. You can use this technique to keep you in the moment while practicing a creative activity like drawing or painting, but you can apply it to any creative task. The other benefit is it will make you feel more alert and aware of your presence when you are going about your daily routine.

Exercise 3. Active mindfulness

Practice mindfulness next time you get up in the morning. While you are showering, try to be conscious of all the senses of showering. Feel the soap on your skin, the warmth of the water, the sound of the water running and as it hits the walls. See what the soap does on your body or how it flows over your arms and legs and into the drain. Experience the fragrance of the water and soap too. All the while try to be present and not let your thoughts wander off to future or past events. You might find you can only do it for about 10 seconds before your thoughts run off onto other things. That's ok; keep trying every morning and see if you can be mindful for longer periods. Try it when you are dressing or making breakfast or brushing your teeth too.

In the workbook, use the list of mindfulness examples and try each one for a week. In the space provided list down any thoughts that come up. Is there a common theme that comes up when you do this?

Often this type of exercise creates some resistance in your own mind; you might feel frustrated by the process or feel like you can't dispel your thoughts even for a short while. That's ok. Write down these frustrations and experiences. Each time you do a mindfulness act it will become easier. Eventually you will ease into it in any situation.

Exercise 4. Meditation to enhance creativity

Start by finding a comfortable place to sit. It can be a chair or on a rug on the floor. You can start by doing this meditation for 5, 10 minutes and then 15 minutes. I suggest you have a timer that you can set to these times so you don't have to look at your watch as you're doing the exercise. There are some great apps you can download that give you a nice sounding bell when the time is up.

Close your eyes and become aware of any sensations you might be feeling. It could be any stresses or tensions in your body, or there could be warm or cold sensations – anything that you might be feeling in your body at that moment. Now turn to your thoughts, and see what comes to your mind. There might be emotions and urges coming up too.

Whatever is present, just be aware of those thoughts and emotions as they emerge. As you sit you will notice these thoughts and emotions entering your mind in a constant stream. Unlike mindfulness you don't have do anything other then observe them as they come to you and eventually fade away. You can imagine the thoughts and emotions as leaves slowly floating by on a stream and you are watching them go past one by one.

There's no need to become wrapped up in those thoughts or make any judgements about them; you simply observe them, letting the thought linger in front of you for a while and then letting it continue down stream. When the timer ends, simply open your eyes and get up when you feel ready to do so.

With practice this will become easier and you will find meditation not only enhances your creative thinking, but gives you an overall boost to your well being.

Are you curious?

What's so important about being curious? As adults we accumulate a heap of knowledge over time: like geographical locations, historic events, local information, traffic conditions, weather predictions, friends' addresses and more. All these things help us function normally throughout the day, yet we overlook many little things at the same time. Curiosity is another trait that children possess naturally, but as we grow older that natural curiosity steadily decreases. It's not enough to say 'just be curious'; rather we need to re-acquaint ourselves with that trait we all have inside. And for everyone that process will happen in slightly different ways.

Another key benefit of curiosity for a creative person is that it opens your mind to new ideas and it helps you approach creative tasks or problems with a positive frame of mind. You will seek to discover new possibilities where you would otherwise have given up.

How do you start re-acquainting yourself with curiosity?

Question things. We all take things for granted in this world. Our schooling has taught us everything from how things work to laws of physics, but you should sometimes ask why. Or ask how. Sometimes asking why something is that way or how something came to be that way can be the opening to a new idea.

Avoid routine. This is the most valuable thing you can do to enhance your curiosity. When you do the same thing every day or settle for a routine because you 'don't have to make any decisions' you are eliminating the need to be curious. Once you break from a routine, however small, your mind begins to observe and be curious about the new experience.

Avoid boredom. This one is closely linked to the one above. Routine breeds boredom and so your curiosity is diminished with it. When you lose interest in something then boredom sets in and can be hard to shake. By giving yourself new challenges and new things to learn, your curiosity will rise to the occasion once more.

Become an explorer. You can increase your curiosity when you explore your surroundings. Especially if you are breaking your routine and thus breaking boredom all at once. Exploring your local streets on a morning walk, or exploring cities or new countries are all ways of heightening curiosity.

So, here's an example of how you can adopt this method to re-acquaint yourself with curiosity. If you walk to a train station in the mornings, you can observe things along the way; for example house fences. Or it could be other things that might present themselves in your particular part of the world. Something mundane like this example can actually be very interesting when you focus on it. Where curiosity becomes important is that normally you might notice homes with different fences for example, but when you are actively curious, you will start to notice various details such as wood textures, paint colors, weathering of some fences over newer ones, or you'll see some fences made of stone or bricks laid in odd patterns. It's amazing what you notice when you are being actively curious about something.

Exercise 5. Awakening your curiosity

Instead of going the usual way to work one morning, take an alternate route. Or you can try and go home a different way.

Listen to people's conversations in a cafe. I know this seems a little invasive, but we've all done it before, even if we don't like to admit it. I'm not asking you to push your chair closer to the quarrelling couple in the corner and nod in approval or tsk tsk in disapproval with their every word. In fact if you can only hear the odd word or sentence, that's even better as it will make your brain try to fill in the other parts of the conversation. It's amazing how one line taken out of context can awaken all sorts of ideas in your own mind.

Take an everyday object in your home and try to find out something about it you never knew. This will require you to ask questions like where was it made? Who first invented it? Why was it made this way? It could be a drinking glass, and if you're thinking that's a boring item to use, then all the better. The idea is to use your curiosity to open up all sorts of new possibilities. It's ok to go to Google for this one. Or perhaps you can try to get the answers to your questions by only asking other people. Now there's a real challenge!

Check out the workbook for a few fun phrases to get you started.

By now you have seen how important it is to have your mind in the right place. We all have negative thoughts once in a while, but now you know how to keep those thoughts at bay and encourage positive ones.

In preparing your mind you have practiced mindfulness in your routines and perhaps seen how your thoughts have become clearer too. When we practice mindfulness over a period of time we can be calmer in moments of stress and thus make better decisions. Your meditation will also enhance that decision-making process and your clarity of thought.

In the next chapter you'll start with one of the most important things you need before you do any creative work and it doesn't involve picking up a paintbrush, yet. It's about getting your space right for your work. You will discover how to give it that personal touch so that when you sit down to work you will be in the right zone for creativity.

STEP 2

CREATE YOUR SPACE

Creativity is allowing yourself to make mistakes. Art is knowing which ones to keep.

– Scott Adams

YOUR SPACE

Now you've had time to open yourself up to creativity your ideas might already be flowing. That's great! In this chapter you will learn about setting yourself up in a space that will give you the best opportunity to be creative.

Make space for your creativity

The first thing you need is a physical space. Not only is this a practical thing on which to put your paper or pencil, it is about helping you get into the creative mindset. That way when you sit at your dedicated space, your mind will already be getting into that creative mode. Artists have used studios to be creative for hundreds of years, and while your space doesn't have to be too elaborate it does need to have some fundamental things. It can be a desk in the corner, an entire room or a bench in a shed if need be. Or it could be as simple as the dining table that you occupy for a period of time. The important thing is to have this space available when you need it and not feel like you are encroaching on someone else's space.

Some options for setting up your space

A desk

You can set up a desk in a room, hopefully with the ability to shut yourself away from any distractions. Make sure it's clear of any other household items, (for example kids' laptops, books or storage boxes), and make sure everyone in your household knows this space is now off limits to anyone but you. The desk should be large enough to accommodate an A3 sketchbook and some paints or pencils. We will go into more detail on the materials you will need further into the book.

It's also important that you can leave your work in progress on the desk without fear of someone tampering with it, or a pet chewing it while you're out of the room. This may not be possible, but it really helps when you're in the middle of developing a project that you can leave it in full view for a day or more. When the project is visible it will be on your mind and your subconscious will be working away at some ideas even if you don't realise it.

Dinner table

This one is for those of you who have limited space available. A dinner table can be a workable solution provided you approach your work with a little more preparation. First thing is to find a cloth or table covering that will protect the table from any spills. Or you can use a big piece of vinyl you can roll on and roll off when needed. Vinyl can be purchased at most hardware stores by the metre. You should keep your pencils, brushes and paints in small storage boxes so you can easily bring them out when needed.

The dedicated room or shed

If you have a spare room or shed, then this is a great way to start. Although all of the exercises in this book are tailored to complete in small spaces, having a room to use only for your creative pursuit is a wonderful luxury. Depending on the size of your room or shed, you can place a bench against a wall and have floor space to put down larger papers or canvases. Consider placing shelving on a wall to give you quick access to materials. You could even paint one wall a vibrant color to fill the space with some energy. Be aware that this type of setup has many more options to list here and can be a creative project in itself. Whichever way you decide to go with your setup it shouldn't take up all your spare time and be a burden. The idea is to have somewhere practical to work and get on with your creativity.

Inspiration board

A handy thing to have is a board where you can stick lots

of inspiring things along the way. You can purchase cork boards from hardware or art and craft stores. If you are setting up a desk then you can place it in front of your work area and have it visible at all times. You can cover it in linen or coloured cloth to make it a little more special too.

Use your inspiration board to pin notes, inspiring photographs or quotes from artists you admire. Just remember not to fill up all the available space yet – it will be a handy tool as you progress through your projects and want to pin things that you like or feel proud of.

It also works really well as a place to reflect on things you are working on. If you find you're getting stuck on a drawing you can pin it up and leave it there while you work on something else. After a while you can look back on it and you might see exactly why it was not working for you.

All in good measure

The next two sections of this book are where you really get into gear. You've got yourself thinking the right way and you have a place to work that's your own, whether it's a desk or a shed out the back.

This book is structured into two main parts: Inspiration and Perspiration. The key to bringing out your own creative power is to use techniques and tips from both these areas.

It is important to read the Inspiration section first as a way of getting yourself stimulated and motivated. It will show you proven ways of developing inspiration and how to keep your inspiration well from running dry.

STEP 3

CULTIVATE INSPIRATION

Creative work is not a selfish act or a bid for attention on the part of the actor. It's a gift to the world and every being in it. Don't cheat us of your contribution. Give us what you've got.
— Steven Pressfield

INTRODUCTION TO INSPIRATION

'Finding your muse' or 'getting a spark of an idea', 'getting the creative juices flowing' are familiar terms when we think about inspiration. The difficulty is that sometimes when we want to do something creative we come up against a lack of inspiration just when we need it.

We've all been there and it can be very deflating to our creative process and likely to put you off doing anything. So how do you find inspiration? Is there a secret formula that all creative people know about?

The answer is you don't find inspiration, you let inspiration find you. How does this happen? It's about daily habits you develop that, although small and insignificant by themselves, collectively build up a well of inspiration that will be available to you anytime.

So there isn't a secret to it; inspiration will begin to flow and you will feel comfort in the knowledge that you can draw on it when you need it. All those negative associations about being blocked or not finding your muse won't worry you because you will have inspiration at hand.

The following chapters will guide you through some techniques I and many other creative people have used, whether they are painters, photographers or writers.

The best thing of all is that it's not about doing hard work; it's about discovery and enjoying things you like. One thing that people often misunderstand when they look at artists or creative types, is they think artistic people somehow have a special talent for coming up with ideas out of nowhere, where in fact, their ideas always come from somewhere. It can be that postcard you found in a cafe, or the quote your wrote down on a train one day; all of these things go into the inspiration well until one day something else connects inside you and you have the start of a creative idea. Now that you are open to let creativity into your life, this part will feel very natural.

Galleries and Exhibitions

Some of the easiest places to start getting inspired are galleries. It's the most obvious and simplest of ways to see what other creative people (in this case artists) are doing. It's time to get reacquainted with galleries in your city if you haven't already. These are places where art and creative ideas are on display all year round.

Why are these places great for inspiration? The first thing is you have to get out of your environment to get there. The bigger galleries are often in a city, which means the travel there provides stimulation to the senses. The buildings themselves are often designed in bold and interesting architectural ways so when you enter through the front doors your mind is prepared to absorb new things.

The bigger art galleries often have temporary exhibitions that might showcase a particular artist, or group of artists. They might be showing works from a particular era or genre. Take note of these things, and see if there are artists or styles that attract you more than others. Be open to seeing the type of art that might not be your favourite style too.

Now that you are open to creativity you should be open to viewing new things that may not always be to your taste. If you have always liked landscapes, see an Abstract exhibition: or if you like paintings from the Renaissance period, see works from the Modern era.

Apart from the big art galleries, you should consider smaller galleries. These are often private galleries that might not have as many artists on show, but might have a certain style of artwork you admire. Have a look in your local area for touring exhibitions that didn't make it into the big art galleries, and you might find something very interesting.

Be on the lookout for all types of art forms when you are visiting galleries: for example tapestry, sculpture, pottery, fashion, furniture, silver smithing, projections, glassware can all give you inspiration. All of these types of works offer you insight into how other people create things and might change the way you see your own project.

Exercise 6. Visiting galleries

Visit one major exhibition in your nearest city. In your worksheet, take note of what impressed you about the exhibition. Answer the following questions about it:

What was the theme of the exhibition?

What mediums were used primarily? Paint, sculpture, other?

Were there any works of art that gave you ideas? Describe those pieces of art.

Study an artist

As you begin to visit more and more galleries you will discover new artists. Learning about an artist will help you learn how they use a medium like painting or sculpture to create something new and exciting. Or show you a progression of a theme over the course of the artist's life work.

Finding inspiration in an artist is very helpful to your own creativity. All artists have interesting lives and their work often springs from their life experience. There is a myth that all artists are tortured artists or are weird people. Maybe because we hear about artists like Van Gogh who led a tragic life. You don't need to be a tortured artist to live a fulfilling creative life.

The 20th century was an enormously creative period in the art world. Even though there were two world wars, or maybe because of it, artists started looking at the world in a different way. Many of them let go of the traditional forms of painting and began experimenting with color and form, what beauty was and the medium itself.

Picasso is a great example of an artist who experimented with new styles of art and dedicated his whole life to being creative by using many mediums like painting, sculpture, drawing and print making.

Find an artist from the last century by searching online or by looking at books in an art bookstore. Buying books on art is a fantastic way of getting inspiration.

I can wander for hours amongst the shelves of bookstores looking for new books on art and design.

Exercise 7. Discover an artist

See if you can answer the following about your chosen artist:

What medium do they use primarily?

What themes can your see in their work? (Is it about the female form, love, a new way of describing the world)?

Are there any quotes from them that inspire you?

Become a collector

While you are out and about visiting galleries and seeing new artists you should be on the lookout for things to collect. Becoming a collector is a vital part of developing your inspiration well. You can imagine this as a treasure hunt of sorts. Instead of looking for clues, you are finding things that will uncover your own inspiration. This should become part of your everyday routine. Anywhere you are, whether it's a park, cafe, supermarket, library or gallery, all these places offer you something you can collect.

Items to collect are too numerous to list here but to give you some guidance here are a few things that are often great sources of inspiration.

- Postcards
- Greeting cards
- Packaging labels, especially foreign packaging seems to have a curious element to it

- Photos, from magazines, or photos you have in a shoebox
- Fabric, with patterns, or a sample of a color you like
- Quotes you find in a newspaper or magazine
- Leaves, almost anything organic such as branches and flowers
- Matchboxes

Exercise 8. Collecting

The next thing is to make use of that pin board you have set up near or in front of your desk. Hopefully you have some room there for your collections. Of course you don't have to fill it up in one go. The collection process should happen in a relaxed way whenever you are out but shouldn't make you feel like you are under pressure to find something. It will be something very natural and you won't even realise it when you are peeling a label off a bottle at a restaurant to take home.

So be on the lookout this week for something that catches your eye. Find at least one thing you can pin on your board.

Music as inspiration

Music has a powerful effect on us all. Apart from making us move on a dance floor, we use it in our lives to do the house work, or help us relax from a busy day. Music can inspire deep emotions within us. It can be uplifting and take us to another place. But we can also use that power of music to do something creative. You may be one of those people that listens to music but aren't listening to the words very closely. This next part of the inspiration process will show you how you can harness the words and the emotional power that music has. You will be able to draw out inspiration by listening to music in a purposeful way.

Exercise 9. Listen to music

Find two pieces of music. Firstly, a classical track from someone like Beethoven, Mozart or another classical composer. The second piece can be a folk, country song or any song that has a lot of lyrics, such as a Johnny Cash or Bob Dylan song for example.

Listen to each piece of music while seated at your desk and have a pen and your workbook open at Exercise 9 handy. With the classical piece, just let yourself relax and see what images rise up in your mind as the music flows. It might conjure up very distinct images; make a note of them as they present themselves.

Alternatively the music might bring up emotions; write these down too. If nothing comes up for you immediately, don't force yourself. Just let the music sit with you until something appears, because it will.

When you listen to the second piece of music, the one with lots of lyrics, listen to the messages or stories the lyrics create in your mind. As before, simply sit at your desk or in an armchair and be ready to write down the lyrics that catch your attention.

You will find there will be certain phrases that jump out at you. They could be about love, and probably will be as most songs deal with this theme. But in that short phrase you might hear another meaning that is relevant to you.

This exercise can produce different results for different people as it depends on what you might be feeling or thinking in that moment.

Don't be discouraged if the first attempts don't give you much in the way of ideas or words to write. Eventually the lyrics and music will bring up images in your head that are quite vivid. I have used this technique for writing short stories, sometimes using only three or five words taken from a song and turned the meaning into something quite different that made sense to my story.

You could even type out the line from the song, even if it's out of context (even better in my view) and stick it up on your pin board. You can use this to write in your journal, as a writing prompt or as a theme for your creative project. Try different songs, different genres of music and see what comes up for you.

Go for a walk

How can going for a walk make you more creative? Let me describe why this is such a great thing. Many people know they should have a break while at work, but instead they sit in front of their computer or paperwork because they have an urgent deadline. They toil away not really getting very far and feeling more and more frustrated. Does this sound familiar?

Think of your mind as a child. A child that is always trying to distract you from the task that you know you should be doing, like work or even fun stuff like painting, drawing or writing.

When you leave your project and go for a walk, what you are essentially saying is, 'Ok mind, I'm taking you out for a stroll to keep you happy'. The result is that you settle your mind from the struggle of trying to think of something 'new' which it fights against, and by stimulating it with new senses as you walk your subconscious will actually be busy working away at the creative project.

There's no need to force anything as you walk around: you can touch base with the creative project to see if anything comes up; if not, no problem, keep walking. Even if you return home and think you haven't come up with anything, you will see that you have detached yourself from the project enough to think about it in a new way.

Taking long walks on a regular basis can be a great way to stimulate yourself before getting into the creative project of the day. When I had very stressful days at work and I was under pressure to come up with something creative, I would take time to go for a walk. Sometimes it was just 5 minutes. While I walked I let myself be present in my surroundings, taking note of trees, homes or people on the street. I didn't worry about the creative problem at all. In fact, if it came up in my mind I would gently let it fade away and get back to observing again. When I returned to my desk a solution to the creative problem always presented itself.

Many writers use this method to enhance their writing flow. It seems especially beneficial to the writing process but can be applied to any creative work. So make sure you take time out next time you feel frustrated by a creative project or just can't come up with an idea.

The Sound of Silence

Another important part of your everyday inspiration habit is one of the smallest but most effective things you can do. It's to allow yourself to have moments of silence and stillness. I make a point of mentioning both, because they are connected yet independent things. It might sound trivial and you might think it's not worth dwelling on, but silence itself allows your thoughts to develop and grow into fully formed ideas.

Stillness is about finding a place physically where you can sit and mentally achieve a sense of stillness where your thoughts quieten. When you are having a busy day or week, your thoughts tend to speed up and pass by like a laundry list of 'things to do'. It can be very easy to fall into the habit of reacting to these 'to do' thoughts all the time. If you can break the cycle for just a moment it gives way to your higher thoughts and allows your deeper desires room to work themselves to front and centre, thus your creativity will come easier and be more accessible.

Things you could consider include going to a park on your lunch hour and finding a place to sit in silence for a little while. Arriving at work 15 minutes earlier and finding a place in the office to sit still can be of great benefit. Finding 5 minutes at a time should be achievable in our busy lives. The important thing is to make time for it. Any creative thoughts that might have been at the back of your mind might become clearer during that time.

Exercise 10. Find your silent place

A space for silence and stillness can be anywhere as long as you know it will work for you. This week, look for your place; whether it's at your work place, or a place nearby work, or at home where you can sit in silence. Make sure your cell phone is switched off or on silent for the duration of your time.

Start with 5 minutes in the morning before you rush off to work, or at lunchtime or in the evening. Find the time that suits you best and try to stick to it for 5 days. Do this for 5 minutes, no more, because even those 5 minutes will feel quite long to begin with.

You can do anything you like in those 5 minutes: think about your favourite film, or a book you have been reading or a creative idea that's been floating around your head. Don't write anything or try to work out a complex problem; just let your thoughts go wherever they like, but if your mind starts chattering about all the things you need to do, gently steer it back to the present. Listen to the wind, or the rustle of nearby leaves; very soon you will be back in the moment of stillness.

Although you don't have to write anything at the time of doing this exercise, the Workbook has a space for you to keep track of how you progress with this. It might be good to have a record of places you find that are more successful than others.

You may find this very similar to the meditation exercise earlier in the book. There is a direct link, but the difference here is to keep your eyes open and engage with those thoughts that are the start of an idea. In other words, give them space to bubble to the surface and follow those thoughts to see where they may lead you. Once you have done your 5 minutes you can get back to your busy day again. In this way when you actually sit down to work on your creative project, the idea or ideas will be top of mind.

Find your intuition

How do you explain something we have all experienced, yet it's a sense that exists outside our six senses? It's the type of thing that people describe as a gut feeling or 'somehow I just knew' feeling. That's intuition.

We all know about it 'intuitively'. The experience is a familiar one; we are driving along and suddenly we decide to turn down another road instead of the regular way home. Later we find out an accident occurred on the road you were about to head down before changing your mind at the last moment. The easiest way to describe it is 'thinking without thinking'. It's about making a decision in an instant rather than deliberate rational thinking. And yet somehow we often know that it is the right decision.

As you develop all the facets of inspiration we've been discussing in earlier chapters, your intuition will also develop naturally. As you trust your intuition more and more, so too you will trust the creative decisions you make as you get that 'just feels right' feeling.

Fundamentally, intuition and creativity are almost interchangeable. When both qualities are working together they provide a sense that things just flow, or become effortless. All artists strive for this feeling in their work and you can achieve this in your creative work too.

How do you help it along? The reason this topic is here instead of appearing earlier is because you are already helping your intuition to be stronger without realising it. All those things you've been learning about such as mindfulness, positivity, curiosity, using silence and meditation have been feeding your intuition. How awesome is that?

Whenever you find some time to quieten your mind and sit in silence as described earlier that's helping intuition along. Mindfulness plays a part by keeping you in the present moment – where intuition seems to be at its best. Once you start to worry about future or past events, those thoughts prevent intuition from surfacing.

Exercise 11. Get help from your subconscious

This exercise can be very powerful. Psychologists have studied the subconscious mind for decades. It's still something of a mystery as to how it works in relation to our conscious mind. All we need to know is that it can be a great help and it does its part in building your intuition.

When you go to bed, reflect on questions you may have on a creative problem. It might be ideas you have been developing and need a solution. You can actually speak to your subconscious much like you speak to a friend.

Try saying to your subconscious: 'Hey subconscious, I need help with…'. Make the problem or question clear. Repeat it once or twice in the same way. There are a couple of reasons why you need to repeat it. Firstly, your subconscious needs to be aware this is important. There are lots of things it's working on in the background – similar to a background application on your computer that's always running.

Secondly, when you speak to it directly and repeat the issue or question, it's like bringing that application to the foreground and making sure it knows what you need in no uncertain terms.

Keep a notebook and pen by your bedside because you never know when your subconscious will come back to you with an answer.

I have used this technique over the years for various creative solutions and am always amazed at how it works. The answer comes at any time and usually in the middle of doing a very mundane task. When you experience it for yourself you will come to see it as a great resource too.

Talk about it

Giving voice to your creative thoughts is another way of encouraging your inspiration. Quite literally speaking to someone, whether it's a friend, family member or colleague, can be the push you need to get started. There are many ways to approach this and I've found that sometimes talking to people that are not creative gives you the most interesting insights.

Firstly, they are looking at things from the outside and they have no emotional attachment to what you are creating. Those two things can often hinder you from moving forward with a project or idea. If you are too close to your work, then you will find it hard to make decisions about what is relevant and what isn't, while speaking to someone who knows nothing about your work can give you a fresh perspective.

How do you do this? Firstly you need to find the right person that you can talk to on a regular basis so you can go back to them over the course of a few days or weeks. It should be someone you trust and have a good rapport with. Secondly, there are two scenarios: to have a verbal discussion about an idea or get their feedback from a piece of your work.

In this section we'll focus more on the verbal discussion, because we want to focus on the inspiration part first.

Once you find that person you can begin to tell them about your ideas or what's been on your mind. Leave the topic open for the other person to give their opinion or contribute to what you have said. This shouldn't be an interrogation. The ideal situation is to develop a dialogue with a person that you feel relaxed with so that your initial idea or thought bubble can grow into something bigger. That's why it's important to have a good rapport with that person so you don't feel judged but instead be encouraged.

Remember, if they go off on a tangent when they hear about your idea don't try to stop them or steer them back to your train of thought. You have to be as open and non-judgemental as you want them to be. You never know; that tangent might give you inspiration to change or develop the project in new ways. It might inspire them in the process, and that's a great thing too.

Ways of starting that dialogue can be saying things like: 'I've been thinking about doing X Y Z, what do you think about it?' Or 'I would like to do X Y Z, how would you do it?'.

If you can have a consistent dialogue with the same person or several people over time you will find this is an invaluable tool to flesh out ideas or nut out creative projects that are not going anywhere.

I've found that speaking to people from all walks of life has given me crucial insights just when I needed them. Sometimes they have suggested small things that I had completely overlooked but that made all the difference to my project in the end.

As well as having a way of bouncing off ideas with, they provide another often overlooked function. That is, they can hold you accountable for your progress. It might be great to have that initial inspiration to get started, but sometimes no matter how enthusiastic you were in the beginning, seeing the project through to the end is not easy.

This is where your person can ask you about that project you are working on, or how you are going with that idea. You can even ask them when you first start your dialogue to remind you about the project and keep you accountable. Sometimes just speaking out loud to someone about your ideas can be a great motivation.

Getting feedback

Let's discuss briefly how you approach showing your work to someone. The goal here, unlike the open verbal discussion, is to get more specific comments from them. You actually don't want to have an open dialogue when it comes to them commenting on your work. For example you could end up with too many things they suggest you change in your painting and that won't be helpful.

What things shouldn't you say?

The worst thing you can ask of someone is, 'Is this any good?' Or, 'Do you like this?'. In this situation you will most likely get one type of answer. If they are a friend or family member they will of course say that they love it or that's it's fantastic and beautiful. Most likely they wouldn't be brutally honest and tell you they thought the painting was not very good. On the other hand, if they happen to be the type of person that is brutally honest and tell you they don't like your work, then that doesn't help you either.

So, the best way to get feedback is to ask specific things like: 'What do you think of the background?' or, 'Do the flowers' petals look realistic?' or, 'Which of these two pieces grab your attention more? Why?'. Do you see how all of the above questions give the person clear boundaries in which to give their feedback? They might say they don't like the background, but then you can ask why and you will get specific answers like they happen to not like the blue color or that it's too bright and overpowers the rest of the elements.

By now you should be in a great space of feeling positive and energised about creating new things. You may have visited a gallery and found some things on your walks or picked up an interesting flyer in a cafe. And you may have been having some inspiring conversations with a friend or colleague. In the next chapter you get to test out some of those practices. You will learn why a journal can be so important to your creative life. You'll learn how you can bring the creative exercises and the mindfulness technique together to really enhance your practice.

It's time to pick up a pencil and get to work! Let's put inspiration into practice!

STEP 4

PERSPIRATION

Painting must be fertile. It must give birth to a world.. ..it must fertilize the imagination.

— Joan Miro

INTRODUCTION TO PERSPIRATION

You might have heard the saying 'genius is 1 percent inspiration, 99 percent perspiration.' That saying by Thomas Edison has always been important to me and has helped me be realistic about the creative process; especially when I've tried to work on a new idea that just doesn't seem to want to come to me.

What I now know after years of working in a creative industry is more like: 'inspiration and perspiration are present in almost equal measure when you are being creative'. Why? Because inspiration isn't about a single idea that hits you like a lighting bolt one day; it's more like a continuous flow of smaller ideas that are being added one after another into your inspiration well. When and how you connect these smaller ideas is the source of consistent creativity.

By now you should be familiar with the concept of how you keep yourself inspired in your everyday life. You might have visited an art exhibition, collected things that capture your attention, listened to music in a more purposeful way, or read something completely new in a magazine or book. You might have found an artist that you connected with through his or her artwork.

Next you get into some real practices that will make you test the waters of creativity and see which things propel you to follow your own creative venture. Read on to see where to begin.

Journaling

Why is journaling such a great way of unlocking your creativity? In our busy lives we find it hard to connect with the one person we should – ourselves. It's easy to be caught up in the tasks of the day or week and not reflect on what's really going on for ourselves in the present. We have already established other techniques to help you reflect like mindfulness and allowing yourself some silence, but journaling takes this one step further. It helps you create a discussion with yourself that forces things to come to the surface in ways you may not be aware of.

You could describe it as a pin board in written form. Where all those things that are floating inside your head can be 'pinned' or in this case, penned, and kept as a record for future use. Keeping a record of your thoughts, brainwaves or just a conversation is a way of sounding out what's important to you at this moment. In the process your journaling can disclose inner feelings and thoughts that don't reveal themselves just by thinking.

It can help reduce stress. When there are highly emotional things in your life, or someone or a situation has made you angry, you can write about it and release those emotions onto the page, thus calming you and making you feel like you are more in control of those emotions.

Another really good reason to keep a journal is the benefits to your own mental health. It can clarify your thoughts. If you have felt like you have alot of things going on but can't express exactly what you're feeling, then writing down your thoughts and emotions for a few minutes will help clarify things for you

It will help you know yourself better. This is about setting a routine for your journal. Over time as you write, more of your inner motivations will be revealed.

There are so many ways of journaling and each person's method will be different. For the purposes of this book, we want to use a journal to help you be more creative. How do you use it for creative ideas? One of the benefits of journaling is to make you a better observer. By writing down things in detail you look at an event or experience and take note of details you may have omitted if you were recounting the same event to a friend. This is a great skill to develop for your own creativity.

It can inspire you by helping you build on an idea or a thought. Sometimes you may not realise you have the beginnings of something really creative. When you are documenting things in your journal it will keep things in front of you so when you review it later, you might find something in there that will generate a new idea. I see this process as getting things out of your head and onto paper that way you can be free to think up other things. Sometimes it can just be a great relief to write.

Most importantly journaling will nurture your creativity. We sometimes carry around a lot of fears – fear of failure or fear of criticism and fear of rejection. Your journal is a safe haven where you can be completely yourself without fear. You should never edit when you write in your journal, rather you should feel safe knowing this is an area for honest self-expression. This goes to the heart of what a daily creative life is about. When you are able to be emotionally expressive through this form of self-communication your creativity will flow.

Some basic tips to start you on your journaling habit are: take your journal wherever you go and find time during the day when you can write a few lines in it. It can be a small entry if you like. Secondly, be consistent, pick a time frame when you feel comfortable and know it will be do-able. Start with 5 minutes of free writing in the morning for a few days a week. Make sure you don't edit yourself, and keep writing anything that comes to you when you first get up in the morning.

You can build up from there. And lastly, make sure you write by hand and not on your laptop or computer. Although there is software for journaling available, the physical activity of your hand connecting to the paper and seeing the words flow is important to the process. After all you are working on improving your creativity so pen and paper is the best way to do this.

Over the years I have owned many journals. Some I have written in, some I have doodled in and others I have pasted things into. There is no rule to say you can only have one, but it helps to stick to one in the beginning.

Find a journal that you will work with and start today. Below are some prompts to get you going. Try out one or a few of these this week and see which one works best for you. You can always try another in the following weeks. Make an effort to stick with one or two techniques and do it consistently. You might see how it changes the way you think.

What about writing down my dreams? I hear you ask. Aren't dreams creative sources of inspiration too? There is a reason I have left this type of writing out of the creative journal. There are dream journals where people write their dreams to potentially use as a source of creativity. In my experience writing my dreams in a journal has resulted in pages filled with chaotic stories and disconnected emotions and events. I think dreams are fascinating but often they are hard to make good use of in the creative process. I think there is much more value in having a sense of direction when you are doing your journal.

There's no harm in setting yourself rules about what goes into the journal and what stays out of it. You could include your dreams if you feel strongly about their potential to inspire you. As long as you can look back on your journal and see a sense of purpose to your writing. This includes any doodles or sketches that will be an expression of your inner self too.

What you'll need:

A journal with good quality paper. It can be ruled or unruled.

Pen, pencil. Try different colored pencils.

Exercise 12. First thing in the morning journal

As briefly described above, write down anything that comes to you when you wake up in the morning. Time yourself for 5 minutes and see how much you can write. If you feel stuck (and you probably will at first), write about how hard you find it. It will take you a few minutes of writing before you find a flow. Try this exercise consistently for a week then move on to the next exercise. Or you can try this one in the mornings and the other exercises in the evenings.

Exercise 13. Journaling in timed brainstorming

Set a timer for 5 minutes and begin writing down all the ideas that come to you. You can write about photographic ideas, a character study of someone you know, themes of paintings you might do. Get the ideas down quickly and with enough detail that you can review them later and understand what you were talking about, but don't worry too much about how you will do these things. You can write outlandish ideas too; it's about getting down whatever comes to you. Remember, there are no bad ideas when you're brainstorming and you will be the only person looking at them anyway.

Below are a few more ideas on what to include in your journal. Of course, there are many more things. It's a good idea to try a few or all of these exercises before you decide which ones you are going to do consistently.

- Write about your reactions to personal situations
- Interesting, weird or funny things that happened in the week
- Capture significant moments in your life
- Childhood memories - why they were good or bad experiences
- Goals you're working toward
- Inspiring quotes
- Poetry that moves you
- Stick pictures from magazines or photos you love
- Books you want to read
- Jot down things that moved you in a book you've read
- Doodle and draw whatever comes to mind in 1 minute bursts (more on doodling in the next chapter)

Doodling

Out of all the creative practices, doodling is probably the most familiar to all of us. That's why it's a good place to start. Many of us have probably found ourselves doodling in a meeting or while talking on the phone. Often the doodle is a mystery to person who did it. Why did they draw those swirls or triangles for example? And that's exactly the reason doodling is such a great tool to loosen up your creative talents. You are often using your intuition to do it.

I have always enjoyed doodling or as I like to think of it – 'free drawing'. Long before I started writing I would draw in sketchbooks or school exercise books – wherever there was a blank area on paper. There wasn't any real purpose to these doodles; I just went with the flow of ink on paper, adding more and more forms until it felt right to stop. What I didn't realise at the time was that the doodling was keeping my creativity in shape. A bit like regularly stretching in between football matches.

I use sketch books in much the same way now, by starting with any shape that comes to me then adding another shape to it and bit by bit I begin to build a picture. I especially enjoy the discovery aspect of drawing this way. I often have no idea what I am going to do before I start.

Even though doodling can seem overly simple, it can have a powerful impact on the way we process information. As you draw on the page your thinking can become clearer and freer.

As with journaling it's important to let the drawings flow and not edit yourself or stop yourself because you think the drawing is not 'looking good'. It's a great stress release, which is probably why many people doodle in meetings.

There are no rules on how to create a doodle, but the exercises below will give you some guidance to push your doodles into works of art.

What you'll need:
A sketchbook or notepad (no bigger than A4 size)
Pen, pencil or thin marker
Time: 5 - 15 minutes

Exercise 14. Doodling in one line

This is a great exercise and it relies as much on what feels right in your hand as what you see on paper.

Start by putting your pen or pencil somewhere close to the centre of the page and begin drawing smooth lines in any direction. The only rule is your pen or pencil must not leave the paper at any point. Your drawing should be created in one continuous line.

—

It's good to keep your mind free of any ideas of what you want to create. Although it's only natural for your mind to start to think of an end result, try to resist and instead focus on the feel of the lines as they move smoothly around the page. You can work them into loops, or curls or squares and then loops again, as long as you maintain contact with the paper at all times.

Begin with small simple doodles and progress to more elaborate ones where almost the entire page is filled. If you would like to give this exercise a bit more structure, use a timer to set a time limit and see how your doodle changes. Try it for 30 seconds and increase it to a few minutes at a time to see what happens.

Exercise 15. Stick with a shape

In this exercise you pick a geometric shape like a circle, triangle or square and only use this shape on the page. Begin by drawing a triangle in the centre for example and then another triangle intersecting it. The only rule here is to have the shapes intersecting or touching each other whenever you draw a new one. They can be in small rows, inside each other or giant – whichever way feels right to you.

See if you can fill the page with your chosen shape. Try other shapes and see which ones get the more interesting results.

Exercise 16. Say it with flowers

Now that you have loosened up your doodling hand we can move onto something a little more complex. Among the more popular doodles you will come across are floral patterns. It must be something about the beauty and simplicity of flowers that appeals to us all.

Begin with a daisy flower - this can be done by drawing a circle with petals extending from it. Now add a stem with leaves. Add another flower from that stem and try a different flower shape. Keep growing your flowers one from the other to get a free-flowing shape that begins to fill the page. Again, there is no 'right' way to do this; keep drawing and see what happens. If you aren't happy with the look of your flowers, than you can simply start again. The key is to get to a page with lots of free flowing flower shapes. Eventually you will have flowers emerging and unfurling from one another.

You might discover you like drawing flowers in very complex ways with lots of petals and intricate patterns within them, or you might move toward a more abstract form of a flower that is more about repetitive shapes.

Give yourself a bit of time to do this; don't throw in the towel on the first go. Work on this exercise in 15 minute intervals, then leave the sketchpad on your desk for a while and come back another day or when you feel ready again. In this way you won't feel frustrated by the process and want to give up. It's only by doing an exercise like this over an extended time, as simple as it seems, that you get to a result that feels satisfying.

Sketching

Sketching has been a form of depicting our world for centuries. All the great masters in history have created sketches before starting on a painting. The term itself has come to mean a way of outlining an idea before committing to the final thing.

If you are like most people you're thinking, 'I don't know how to draw to save my life'. The surprising thing is most people I've met always have some ability to draw the world around them. It's their ability to observe that is under-utilised. These two things, observation and drawing, are what make a sketch come to life. Here you will learn how to hone your observation skills as you draw. With practice you will notice the details that make a difference from an ok drawing to a great drawing.

The exercises below will start with the simplest way to draw from real life, also known as 'Still Life' and move on from there. By the end of these exercises you will be comfortable with how a sketch is started and what you can do to improve your drawings over time.

What you'll need:

A sketchbook with cartridge or heavy paper. A4 or A3 size are ok to use.

A soft grey lead pencil like B1, B2

Time: 15 minutes

Exercise 17. A simple shape

First you will need to find an object to sketch. Things that don't have complex angles or too much detail work best. A glass, a lamp or an alarm clock are good objects to start with. Place the object on the work area in front of you, but hold on – don't start drawing yet!

Sit for a moment and just observe the object in front of you. Look at the shapes that make up its form. First, see if you can see the contour of its form. Is it long and skinny? Is it rounded? Are there a couple of shapes that make up the form together? This will help you get the first part of the drawing done – the outline.

Begin by putting down some light strokes with your pencil that depict the outline you see. Keep looking back at the object as you sketch, checking back with your outline on paper.

With practice this action will become second nature, but in the beginning it might feel very slow going. Don't give up! The learning of observation, while your hand performs the seemingly complex task of drawing at the same time is a skill that takes practice but it can be learnt.

Once you have your outline down, you should once again sit back and check if it matches the object you are drawing. Don't ponder too much at this point; even if you feel your outline is looking a little wonky, keep the drawing going.

The next stage is about filling in the details you see inside the outline. In the example of the glass, you could draw the rim with the shadows and light that it holds. You could add facets that run along the base, or add the detail of the bottom of the glass, depicting its distorted shape as you view it through the glass.

Once you start working on these details, you will realise how much detail is in a simple object like this. Depending on the light, or shadows, or the objects around it, a glass can have lots of things for you to explore.

Try to draw the same object a few times, whether it's exactly in the same setting or in different lighting, to see how your drawing and ability of observation improves.

Exercise 18. Fruits and things

The fruit bowl is a famous subject for many painters in history. It's easy to set this up on your work table and explore a few things together like fruit, bowls, table cloth. Or you could try pottery, flowers and plants. Set up a group of objects that can be left unmoved for a day or so, as you might like to revisit your subject a few times over the course of a week.

The principle is the same as in the exercise above: look at the overall shapes within the objects; often they are rounded, oval or square for example. Begin to roughly depict the outline with your pencil while leaving the inside blank. Relaxing and staying in the present moment is also really important in this exercise and it will help with the other really important skill needed – your power of observation.

How do the objects relate to each other? What clues do you see that let you know one object is in front of the other? Questioning what you see can help you see details in an object you might have otherwise ignored because you assume a lot of things when you are familiar with a scene like this.

Once you have sketched your fruit still life once, try it again with a timer set at 10, 5 and 2 minutes. It might seem too little time, but it will help you sketch the essence of what you see. It will help loosen up your drawing by forcing you to make quick intuitive decisions and in case you haven't realised it yet, anytime you are using intuition or are working with mindfulness is a great thing.

Exercise 19. Real life

Once you have worked with simple objects the next step is to draw a natural scene. These could be beach scenes, street scenes, landmark buildings like museums, historic buildings or parks. All of these have great features and details you can sketch. All you need is a sketchbook and your favourite pencils and pens.

To start with, choose a place where you can select a simple scene, that is, don't choose a busy city location where people are walking in front of you all the time. Decide what is your main subject: for example if you are in a park with a fountain, you could use the fountain as the main focus. Or in a city square, it might be a sculpture or a prominent building, then the other elements are drawn in less detail around it.

Remember, this is a sketch, so you shouldn't be worried about depicting everything you see in front of you. You can make the drawing as rough as you like, and show only a small part of the entire scene.

The method is much the same as in the previous exercise: work with the outline of the building, observe closely while you sketch and check the proportions are correct as you go. If you want to show more depth you can add some perspective by sketching in any elements that lead you into the main subject. It could be a footpath, benches, tiles, trees for example. The final part of the sketch should be the details. Add anything you see inside your subject. Look at shadows and highlights and see how they define areas within your subject.

Real life sketching can be a great hobby and very addictive. It's a great exercise to get you out of the house and experience places where you might have driven or walked past, and it's a relaxing way to spend an afternoon too.

Collage

Hopefully on your walks you have been finding lots of little treasures by now. If you haven't collected much, don't worry because the first exercise is simple and you should have all the materials lying around the house.

Collage or mixed media is another way of expressing your creativity without using drawing or painting as the main form of art. So if you have struggled to draw or paint in the past this might the best form to use for you.

Artists have been using these techniques for many years. There are some great examples in works by Rauschenberg and Man Ray. Once you have completed these exercises, look up these artists online and see what they have created.

Collage allows you to do what other media can't do. That is to convey an idea using borrowed images. The most memorable and creative uses of collage are ones where the images themselves are used out of context to what they were originally intended. For example an old newspaper clipping of a woman in lingerie placed next to a nuclear bomb might say something totally different than if you saw each photo separately.

What you'll need:
A newspaper. Old newspapers are even better for this purpose
Brown cardboard (the type from a grocery store box or similar)
White card
Scissors or craft knife
Glue

Exercise 20. Collage pieces

In this exercise it is all about getting you familiar with the medium and seeing what works best for you. It deliberately restricts you so you are forced to concentrate on working creatively rather than focusing on colors or spending too much time on collecting materials before you start.

Start by cutting the cardboard box into rectangles roughly 8 x 6 inches (or 20 x 15 cm). You will probably need 3-5 pieces to start with. Make sure you have some left over scrap cardboard for you to use later.

Now flip open your newspaper and scan the pages for a photo that you like, or feel some emotional connection with. Preferably use only black and white photos for now. When you find something you like, cut it out roughly and put it to one side. In fact, I would suggest tearing it out with your fingers for a better effect. Keep doing this until you have a nice pile of photos.

The next step is to find words to go with your pictures. Go back to your newspapers and scan the headlines and articles for words or sentences that catch your eye. By now your mind might already be making a connection between the photos you have and the words you're seeing.

Let your intuition guide you as you decide which words to tear out. If nothing jumps out at you don't worry; just cut out or tear out phrases and words as you come across them. Put them in a separate pile.

Now take one of the cardboard rectangles; you can work with it in a landscape or portrait way. Take a photo from the pile and place it on the cardboard, followed by a cutout of a word or sentence. Play around with the placement of the two things until you're happy with the arrangement. Stick these two onto the cardboard.

There is no limit to how many words or photos should be placed on your cardboard; that's up to your own creative eye. I usually start with one photo and find a place to stick it down; this way I'm committed to working all the other elements with this one 'anchoring' element.

You can use the white card as an additional 'color' along with your photos and words. Cut it or tear it into a shape and glue it onto your 8 x 6 cardboard then glue photos and words over the top. Similarly you can use torn pieces of the brown cardboard glued over the top of the photos or text for an interesting layering effect.

Try the following combinations:
- Use predominately words and very few images.
- Use photos as your main element and very few letters
- Try to spell out something with separate cut letters
- Use parts of people's photos. For example cut cut only eyes, or only mouths stuck over words.

- Try using color photographs from magazines

The combinations are only limited by your creativity. Once you have completed a few (I would recommend doing at least 5) pick your favourite and pin it to your pin board.

Photography

When it comes to photography, there is an enormous amount of information out there; you only have to do a search online to find pages and pages of tutorials, tips and how-to guides. But how do you make use of taking photos for a creative purpose? Some of you may have already dabbled in photography and understand some fundamentals of photography.

If you don't know anything more than point-and-shoot, then that's ok too. The following exercises are good starting points for the novice and again are designed to help you draw on your intuition and curiosity to get interesting results.

This is an area where there is a huge range of equipment available. Use any camera you feel comfortable with; preferably something you know how to use. You don't want to be distracted by too many features and controls.

What you'll need:

A camera: SLR, compact, digital or analogue, or a camera-phone if you wish

Exercise 21. The story

This exercise will get you out of the house and exploring your surroundings. The idea is to try to take a series of images in a location; whether it's a park, a street, a shopping centre or a skate park and make a story with pictures alone. The term 'story' is used very loosely here, don't get too hung up on trying to create a story that someone will interpret. Choose your location and explore its landmarks, features or anything that stands out to you. Shoot as many photos as you like within 15 minutes.

When you're back home choose 12 images you like the most and best show the location or give you a story about this place. Print them as 4 x 5 prints through your local photo outlet.

Once you have your prints lay them out on your desk and see what arrangements you come up with. Which image looks like a good beginning and what naturally follows that one? Do they work best in a grid of 3 across or two rows of 6? Or in one continuous line of 12 prints? Keep arranging them until you feel satisfied with the flow from beginning to end.

This will help you look at photos in the context of each other, so next time you're out shooting you will have this in mind. It will help you think of photos as part of a theme. For instance, how and where would you shoot the following themes?

- Weekend escape
- The morning rush
- Industrial decay
- Solitude

Exercise 22. Color in vogue

Choose a color and take photos with this as the predominant color in the frame. You could find your chosen color in a sign on the street, the color of a door, or in a flower. Think about scale too; it might be something quite small that has the predominant color. Remember to make that color the main thing that people will see in your photo. This exercise can sometimes be harder than you imagine. But the results can be fantastic. Pick your favourite photo and pin it onto your board.

Exercise 23. Single minded

Similar to the previous one, this time choose a subject and over a period of a week try to shoot only this in 15 minutes at a time. It could be wrought iron fences, bicycles, garden gnomes or leaves in puddles. Pick something specific and you will get better results. This will help train your curiosity and your observation skills. This type of exercise works really well when you fit it into a routine like an early morning walk. That way you get your exercise and creative task done all in one!

If you think you need more than a week to get your photos then extend the time. If so I would recommend not to do this exercise for longer than two weeks, otherwise you could be taking photos forever and think there will always be a better photo around the corner. There is no limit to the amount of photos you should take. It all depends on the subject you choose of course.

Once your time is up print out 10 - 12 images you are happiest with. Lay them out on your desk to compare. Narrow down your selection to 6 images from those and pin them onto your pinboard.

The reason you should whittle down your images in this way is to help your decision making. It might sound strange to take a heap of photos and then end up with only six to show for this exercise, and yet it's creating restrictions like this that improves your creative practice. You often get the best results when you are constrained by some rules.

Painting

Why is painting so good for creativity? Above all the other mediums such as drawing or collage, painting is the one medium through which most artists choose to express themselves. It might be because painting gives you the widest scope and the widest range of results. It's yet another way of communicating ideas as we've seen with all these techniques; the difference is that painting is the most expressive medium.

It can be therapeutic. The very action of painting can be relaxing and relieve stress. It allows your mind to be free of rational thoughts and when you incorporate mindfulness it is even more rewarding.

Just like the techniques we've discussed, your intuition plays a big part in the activity of painting. It can help you decide what colors to choose, what form to create or how you will compose the subject in the frame.

The act of painting is the ultimate creation activity; that's why this is at the end of the Perspiration section. It covers a vast area that you can explore for many years to come and you will always learn something new.

To begin these exercises you will need only acrylic paints. Although there are many types of paints like watercolor, oil and gouache, acrylics are the easiest paint to learn with.

You can use it dry, wet or add other mediums to change the opacity or thickness of it. It dries quickly and you can paint over it if you make a mistake.

What you'll need:

- Use good quality paints; they don't have to be the most expensive money can buy, a basic set of colors that will give you a range of techniques to work with. Example: primary colors (white, black, red, blue and yellow). Greens, purple, orange, another bright color like hot pink perhaps.

- Brushes: 1 small, 1 medium and 1 large brush in round and flat bristle shapes (if you're not sure, ask your local art shop for recommendations).

- Canvas paper or other heavy paper. At this stage don't worry about using canvases; paper works well for producing lots of trial and error exercises. Once you are familiar with the techniques you can try it out on a canvas.

- Plate for mixing paint

- Sponge or paper towel

- Palette knife (optional)

- Jar for water, cloths for cleaning up

In case you have never painted with acrylics there are some established techniques all artists use. To become familiar with the medium start with the following:

Dry brush: This is simply applying a color with your brush directly onto dry paper. You can try different quantity of paint and see how far you can spread it on the paper.

Wet paint: Brush water onto the paper surface first. Then load paint onto your brush and apply it on the same wet area. You will see the paint takes on a translucent quality. You can add a small amount of water to the paint on your plate and dilute it before applying to the paper.

Dots: Take a small brush with rounded bristles and make a series of dots close together. When you use enough dots in different colors you will start to see how the colors mix on the paper. A great example of an artist who used this was Seurat from a group of artists called the Pointillists. Have a look at his work for inspiration.

Dabbing: Try applying paint onto a sponge and then dab it onto paper. This effect gives interesting results depending on the type of sponge. You can try a paper towel if you don't have a sponge handy.

Splatter: Acrylics are especially good for this technique. If you've had a stressful day at work you can take it out on your painting using this technique. Load a brush with paint and flick it onto the page or surface. Use different brush sizes and different colors to build up a pattern of splatters. Have a look at an artist like Jackson Pollock's paintings and you'll see how far this technique can go. His artwork might not be everyone's cup of tea but he was a master of creating huge paintings by using this technique alone.

Palette knife: For a thick textured finish, the palette knife is the perfect tool. If you don't have a proper artist's palette knife you can use a plastic spoon. Apply the paint with your knife onto the surface and push it around to create texture. This technique is sometimes called impasto. Many artists have used it in the their artwork such as Vincent Van Gough.

Mixing colors: Lastly, when you mix colors you can be creative with the way these colors combine. For example you can partially mix colors with a knife or brush and apply to paper to get a combination of the two colors' streaks.

Exercises to get you started

In case you can't think of where to start with painting, below are a few ideas that are simple for beginners and you can develop further with practice. The reason I would recommend you don't start painting on canvas just yet is because the idea is to explore and experiment with the following exercises. If you start painting onto a canvas right now, you will most likely not want to 'waste' it so you will be more careful with your painting. In the end you might spend too long trying to make things look good and not get the most out of the exercises. When you paint on canvas paper or a thick paper if you make a mistake or don't like what you're doing you can simply rip it out and start again.

Flowers

Because of their simple shape and bold colors, flowers are great subjects for painting. You can use your doodles of flowers you did in the earlier exercises if you want something to start with. Try painting flowers from your own imagination or use real flowers as your inspiration.

Either way, begin with a background color and then paint the stems as lines wavering across the page. Finally you can add the flower petals and details.

Silhouette

Instead of trying to depict details, you can take a silhouette and paint it. Exotic temples from around the world are the perfect subject. This is how you do it. Search online for 'temples at sunset from Thailand' for example, but you could easily replace Thailand with China, Cambodia or Japan and you will get a huge selection of images. You will see the silhouettes have very distinctive shapes so you can easily replicate them in your painting. Start with a wash of color as your background sunset then create the exotic temple silhouette shape over the background color. You can also do this with cities at dusk for a variation on the theme.

Still life

Using your experience from earlier sketching technique you can paint a bowl of fruit, pottery or a combination of objects. Set up your still life on your table or a place where it is in direct sight when painting. Start by sketching the objects as described before on your paper. Now with your paint begin to fill in the shapes with a base color and build up shade and light, layer by layer.

Color exploration

Choose a maximum of only two or three colors and paint them onto your page. Decide which color is your main color before you begin painting. You might apply the paint in washes, dry paint, or with dots. Whichever technique you decide to use, try to stay with the same one for the entire painting. This will help keep a coherence to the overall painting.

Add your main color first. Once you are happy with the amount you've applied, start applying the next color, your secondary color. Now apply the third color (if you have one). Repeat the process from first to third color over and over again until the whole page is covered in your colors. The aim is to explore color and tone. See how well your main color stands out from the painting. Or has it been obscured by the secondary color you chose? This is a great exercise to see how colors complement each other or clash with each other. Artists like Mark Rothko used color in a sublime way.

Abstract

Abstraction can be a stretch for some people. We naturally want to find meaning in shapes and forms, but this exercise is worth doing for anyone trying to bring out the artist within. Start by working the paint around your paper in any way you like. It could be in an oval, or squares or another organic shape, as long as it doesn't represent a figure or real life.

You might find this difficult at first, but once you get beyond the desire to represent real life, you will find the shapes take on their own meaning. I'm sure you have heard the expression upon seeing an abstract painting, 'My five year old could paint that'. Well try it for yourself and you might find it's not that easy.

You can use a textured effect, dry brush or wet technique and keep layering paint to build shapes and forms into your painting. My recommendation with this type of painting is to decide what type of forms you will work with before you start.

Try working with hard edged shapes or flowing smooth shapes for instance and see which one gives you the most satisfying results.

Well done on getting this far! No doubt you have been getting your hands dirty and worked up some perspiration too, (at least I hope you've made a mess with some of the exercises, otherwise you might be working too carefully). Let's take a moment to reflect on what you've done. By now you should have created a few doodles and maybe you have doodled in your journal too.

You have tried sketching objects around your house, or got out and sketched some real life – fantastic! The collage exercise may have brought out some of your collecting skills and made you look at composition and how to juxtapose images to make something new and interesting. You have some photographs in your collection that are either telling a story, or show one subject in many images or you have a series of awesome photos with a single color as your theme. And finally you have tried your hand at painting in various forms using a variety of techniques.

All these exercises have helped bring out your creative talents. You might have discovered things about how you work that you didn't know beforehand. You will find that some results really stood out to you and made you want to try doing it again and again.

Perhaps you found that some exercises were difficult to achieve and you didn't find the results very satisfying. Before you dismiss those exercises outright, take a moment to reflect on what was particularly hard about it. Were you disappointed with your drawing results? Or maybe your photos just didn't look impressive enough? Often we can be our own worst critic, remember to keep in mind you are exploring creative pursuits right now and have more to explore. And in any case, there is no benchmark you are aiming at other than your own personal satisfaction.

In the next chapter you will see how you can keep the momentum with your creative lifestyle. Now that you've had practice and set the foundations with different creative exercises what do you do with this knowledge? Read on to see how to bring it all together.

STEP 5

STAY ON YOUR PATH

*An idea that is developed and put into action is
more important than an idea that exists only as
an idea.*

– Edward de Bono

BRINGING IT ALL TOGETHER

If you're reading at this point you can now say you are leading a creative life. It doesn't matter how much or how little time you devote to this lifestyle, the important thing is you have started doing it. All you need to do is keep going in the same direction.

Let's summarise what you've learnt:

You've developed a positive attitude

You stopped watching TV (at least for a little while)

You've tried out mindfulness techniques

You've been curious

You have a space that's just for your creative work

You've visited galleries and exhibitions

You may have discovered a new artist that inspires you

You've collected fun and interesting things

You've listened to music in new ways

You know when you need to go for a walk to clear your mind

You've found time to sit in silence

Your intuition may be kicking in by now

You've started to speak about your ideas to someone

You journal is part of your daily or weekly routine

You've doodled, sketched and collaged

You've photographed a variety of things and places

You've tried various painting techniques

Wow! That's amazing work. Now let's learn how to make time for yourself and keep that creative work going. How do you make it part of your life without it feeling like a burden or a task? You will see that it is possible to carve out that creative lifestyle that works best for you and find the balance that gives you the fulfilment you've been wanting.

How do you do this? How do you keep track of all the ideas, keep yourself inspired, and set time aside to work on creative projects while doing a 9 to 5 job? Where I've found the most success over the years is keeping a schedule. It might sound weird to do something creative on a timeframe but it really works.

Although most people want to just get on and be free in their creative pursuit, in reality the routine of our normal lives quickly sets in and creativity takes a back seat. Believe me, this is one of the biggest areas where most people fail.

They can speak about their creative ideas till the cows come home and yet never actually start doing it. Or they may start doing something but very quickly they lose that momentum. That's why making time with yourself and putting it down on paper is the best way. You will be glad you did. Eventually it will become a habit you will do without thinking about it.

Before you launch into anything, get out a calendar and look at your week. We've already spoken briefly about doing exercises on a weekly or daily basis, but now it's time to look at things more closely. This is where you need to make some decisions on where you can devote time to your creative lifestyle that fits with all the other things you do too. Some compromises might have to be made. Make this into a positive exercise for yourself: don't feel disappointed if you find you can only devote one hour a week in your schedule. Think of it as a starting point. You can always build up more time as you need it. And believe me, once you have a creative project that inspires you, you will be motivated to find time any way you can.

First thing is to establish a day of the week that you can practice your creative pursuit. It might be a Saturday morning or an evening during the week. Whatever is best for you, set that first in your calendar and make sure others in your family know about it. This should be your priority. Secondly, set times during the week when you will write or draw in your journal. The best approach I've found is to write in your journal first thing in the morning. You could start with a couple of days a week and build up from there. Whatever the day and time you decide, try to stick with it for a few weeks at least, otherwise you won't get much out of it. Be realistic about the days you choose in the beginning that way you don't put yourself under pressure from the outset.

Thirdly, add some days when you will visit galleries or exhibitions and perhaps do something that takes you out of your normal environment. These dates are dependent on other factors and they can be more flexible; nevertheless you should pencil something in so they don't get neglected.

To reinforce it one more time:
- Look at your schedule for a week or month
- See where you can block out time for your creative activity first and foremost
- Set aside time to work on your journal
- Finally, make note of upcoming exhibitions or galleries you will visit and book them in.

- AND you can also get example creative schedules from the Creative Reboot Workbook if you're feeling stuck

It's good to look back

Once you have scheduled time for your creativity it leaves you free to do the work. So why should you look back? You might be thinking, 'that was fun', and go back to your normal everyday lifestyle. And if you do that's perfectly ok. For the rest who now feel like they are taking control of their creative lifestyle, you sense there is something more rewarding to come.

This is where the your creative lifestyle really begins. Like a lot of creative people do as part of their normal routine, it's a good idea to look back and reflect as well as look to the future. It gives you perspective and insight – two things that really develop your skills.

That's why your journal is a great tool to have and keep working on consistently. When you look back on the early things you put into it, you will see your own progression, which is very satisfying and ultimately encouraging.

You will also build on what you already know. As you progress with your journal, collages, paintings or whatever you decide to keep working with, you will build on those skills and new ideas will organically develop from there.

All successful creative people have worked in this manner. The key is consistency. When you start with an idea, work on it for a period of time. Use your learnt skills to explore it and leave it alone for a while then revisit again.

Finally, looking back on your older ideas, whether they are in your journal or pinned to your board, can create a connection with something in a new way. For example you might have taken photos of those wrought iron fences months ago and pinned them onto your board. One day you are looking through your journal and writing down some possible ideas for a new project, (lets say it's an idea of painting people portraits), but you aren't sure how best to depict them, you see the wrought iron fence photos and make a connection – maybe the fences could be a great device to use in all the paintings – you could paint each person leaning against their home fence!

Other quick tips to keep you going

Remember to talk to friends or colleagues about your creative pursuits and see if they bring anything new to the mix. Or if you need a push get a project finished, tell them what you are doing and when you want to finish it by. This a great way of giving you a push to finish something when your friends hold you accountable by saying, 'How's that project going?'. I've used this technique a few times to finish something.

Sit down every week to go through the ideas you have collected in your journal and sift through them, tossing out the ones that you haven't got time for, and concentrating on the ones you do. Make sure you take a break too. It's wonderful to get involved in your project but you need to know when to walk away and let your mind relax and you will see when you come back to your task it will be ready to go again.

You might find that sketching every weekend is very satisfying or going on trips to take photos on the weekends is all you need to do for now. Perhaps collage is your thing and you find you can cut out photos in front of the TV (if you have started watching it again of course). Or doodle in a sketchbook on the train. Take a life drawing class on a weeknight to break up your routine. Read the bonus projects list at the end of this book for more ideas.

Whichever way you choose to go, the key is to keep doing it consistently. Try to work to your schedule and keep yourself inspired by practising the methods outlined earlier. When you start to work this way for a length of time you will see progress and with every new project you finish you will gain new confidence and feel that inner satisfaction that only being creative can give.

Most importantly, now that you have set yourself on this path don't wait for that perfect moment to be creative. Go forth, be brave and immerse yourself in your creative life right now. You have all the right tools to keep going.

The next chapter is a bonus chapter just to prompt you to start on a project today. These are just a teaser and I'm sure you could think of many more. Turn the page and get started on one today!

BONUS PROJECT IDEAS TO KEEP YOU GOING

- Work at small-scale: cut paper into playing card size rectangles. Now create a work of art using whatever medium you like within this space. Try to do a different one for every day of the week.

- Paint a self-portrait.

- Create a collage at the end of every week and use things you found from that week only.

- Make a board game by drawing and painting the board and making playing pieces from painted wooden pieces.

- Take a photo of an object that has sentimental value (How can you photograph it to show that quality?).

- Take an ordinary small object and draw it so it is out of scale. For example a clothes peg or paper clip as big as a house or building.

- Make gift cards from your doodles on colored card.

- Sketch pine cones, chestnuts or other tree seeds you can find.

- Take photos of sunsets for a week from the same location.

- Paint colored backgrounds into your journal and draw inspiration quotes on them in black marker.

- Write an entry in your journal about your week as if it were a short story.

- Print on a series of squares of wood and use as wall décor.

- Draw your own hand.

- Pick an artist you like and try to replicate their style by painting or sketching.

- Choose a font you like from a newspaper or your computer and draw it large on a canvas and paint it in colors that complement the style of font.

- Doodle patterns in thin marker pen on brown paper.

- Doodle waves and clouds on colored paper and use them as gift-wrapping paper.

ACKNOWLEDGMENTS

I would like to acknowledge the encouragement
I have received over the years from my family, especially my mother. Throughout that time the following people have provided encouraging words, discussions and invaluable support: Andrea, Caroline, Marjel, Renata and Sky.

Thank you.

Thank you for purchasing this book. I really appreciate your feedback and I love hearing what you have to say.

Creativity never stops so I need your input
to make the next version better.

Please leave a helpful REVIEW on Amazon today.

Thanks so much!
Osvaldo

www.ingramcontent.com/pod-product-compliance
Lightning Source LLC
Chambersburg PA
CBHW061441180526
45170CB00004B/1501